BEHIND THE NEWS

UPRISINGS IN THE MIDDLE EAST AND NORTH AFRICA

Philip Steele

CRABTREE
Publishing Company
www.crabtreebooks.com

Crabtree Publishing Company
www.crabtreebooks.com
1-800-387-7650

Published in Canada
616 Welland Ave.
St. Catharines, ON
L2M 5V6

Published in the United States
PMB 59051, 350 Fifth Ave.
59th Floor,
New York, NY

Published in 2017 by CRABTREE PUBLISHING COMPANY.

First published in 2014 by Wayland
(A division of Hachette Children's Books)
Copyright © Wayland 2014

Author: Philip Steele

Contributing writer and indexer: Janine Deschenes

Editorial director: Kathy Middleton

Editors: Emma Marriott, Jon Richards, Ellen Rodger, and Janine Deschenes

Designer: Malcolm Parchment

Proofreader: Wendy Scavuzzo

Production coordinator and prepress technician: Ken Wright

Print coordinator: Katherine Berti

Printed in Canada/072016/PB20160525

Library and Archives Canada Cataloguing in Publication

Steele, Philip, 1948-, author
Uprisings in the Middle East and North Africa / Philip Steele.

(Behind the news)
Includes index.
Issued in print and electronic formats.
ISBN 978-0-7787-2589-3 (hardback).--
ISBN 978-0-7787-2594-7 (paperback).--
ISBN 978-1-4271-1771-7 (html)

1. Revolutions--Middle East--History--21st century--Juvenile literature. 2. Middle East--History--1979- --Juvenile literature. 3. Middle East--Politics and government--1979- --Juvenile literature. 4. Arab Spring, 2010- --Juvenile literature. I. Title.

DS63.123.S75 2016   j956.05'4   C2016-902558-6
                                              C2016-902559-4

Library of Congress Cataloging-in-Publication Data

Names: Steele, Philip, 1948- author.
Title: Uprisings in the Middle East and North Africa / Philip Steele.
Description: New York : Crabtree Publishing, 2016. | Series: Behind the news | Includes index.
Identifiers: LCCN 2016016655 (print) | LCCN 2016021026 (ebook) | ISBN 9780778725893 (reinforced library binding) | ISBN 9780778725947 (pbk.) | ISBN 9781427117717 (electronic HTML)
Subjects: LCSH: Revolutions--Middle East--History--21st century--Juvenile literature. | Middle East--History--1979---Juvenile literature. | Middle East--Politics and government--1979---Juvenile literature. | Arab Spring, 2010---Juvenile literature.
Classification: LCC DS63.123 .S74 2016 (print) | LCC DS63.123 (ebook) | DDC 956.05/4--dc23
LC record available at https://lccn.loc.gov/2016016655

CONTENTS

Changing

A history

Unrest a

Tunisia,

Behind

Dictato

Egypt,

Is den

Faith

Libya

Relig

Saud

CHANGING TIMES

Sometimes, in order to keep power, governments are harsh, controlling, and **oppressive** to their own citizens. Public protests and uprisings are two forms of **resistance**, where a country's people press for change. The goal is to persuade or force the government to give up power so it can be replaced by a government that reflects its citizens' values.

Arab Spring

Many **revolutions** happened across Europe in 1830 and 1848, and again when the **Cold War** came to an end in 1989. Later, from 2010 on, ideas of revolution and change swept across southwest Asia—a region usually known as the Middle East—and North Africa. The series of uprisings became known as the "**Arab Spring**"—although not all the people involved were Arab.

Arab Spring began in Tunisia with a single act of protest by Mohamed Bouazizi (see page 10). Soon, one extraordinary event followed another. It became difficult to control or predict the outcome. Changes are still taking place throughout the region today. News coverage often includes images of violence and fleeing **refugees**. No one can be sure how the uprisings, revolts, and revolutions will end.

Egyptian protestors gather in the city of Alexandria, Egypt to demand the resignation of the then-president Hosni Mubarak.

Making sense of it

This book goes behind the news and asks important questions. What effect does change in the Middle East and North Africa have on the rest of the world? Why are these changes happening now? Who is taking part and what do they want? Which other countries are influencing events? Can the hopeful spirit of people pushing for change continue?

TIDE OF CHANGE

- **Governments overthrown:** Egypt (twice), Libya, Tunisia, and Yemen
- **Wars:** Libya and Syria
- **Protests leading to government changes:** Kuwait, Morocco, Oman, and Palestine
- **Protests:** Algeria, Bahrain, Djibouti, Lebanon, Mauritania, Saudi Arabia, and Sudan
- **Related crises:** Iran, Iraq, Israel, Mali, Turkey, and global refugee crisis

"I think that all of us share and cherish the idea of being free and not afraid anymore."

Nouha Tourki, a teacher from Tunisia, 2011

A HISTORY OF UPRISINGS

The Middle East and North Africa is a crossroads for Asia, Africa, and Europe. It has always been a region of trade, commerce, and many religions and ideas. Many of today's problems are rooted in the area's rich and restless history, including **imperialism** and **colonialism**.

Empires and religions

• Between about 9500 and 2250 B.C.E., the region saw the rise of civilization, farming, cities, and great empires.

• Three religions developed in Western Asia between about 1300 B.C.E. and 632 C.E.—Judaism, Christianity, and Islam.

• Arab empires spread Islam across the region from the 600s to the 1200s. From 1096 to 1303, there were Crusades—"holy wars" between Muslims and European Christians.

Defeated Christian soldiers, known as Crusaders, lay down their weapons to the victorious Muslim leader Saladin.

The Ottoman Empire

• In 1453, a group of Turkish people called the Ottomans captured the city now known as Istanbul. At its height in the 1500s and 1600s, the Ottoman Empire controlled much of Western Asia, North Africa, and Southeast Europe.

• As European nations gained power, the Ottoman Empire went into decline. In the 1800s and 1900s, France, Spain, Italy, and Britain established colonies—areas or countries under their control—and gained influence over North Africa.

• In 1914, the Ottoman Empire joined with Germany and Austria to fight in World War I. The British helped the Arabic people revolt against Ottoman rule. The Ottoman Empire was defeated in 1918 and lost its foreign territories. In 1922, it was replaced by the Republic of Turkey.

The modern region

• Although the Arab people were promised freedom after World War I, an international agreement meant that the French ruled in Syria and Lebanon, and the British took control in Palestine. Palestine was partitioned, or divided, in 1947 to create a new Jewish state which became known as Israel.

• From the 1920s to the 1960s, the countries of the region struggled to win independence. Some corrupt monarchies, or rules by kings and queens, were swept away, but new dictatorships arose in their place.

• Oil wealth transformed Saudi Arabia, Iran, Iraq, and Libya beginning in the 1960s. From the 1940s on, the region has been repeatedly torn apart by terrorism and by regional and international wars.

Oil fields across the Middle East and North Africa, such as this one in Bahrain, have made many of the region's countries incredibly wealthy.

UNREST ACROSS THE REGION

In 2010, rising prices, unemployment, corruption, and oppression led to many public protests and demonstrations in Tunisia. People wanted the right to vote in fair elections and to speak freely. To everyone's surprise, the power of so many people protesting in the streets proved irresistible. Protest movements sprung up in other Arab countries. The old political systems began to collapse.

A patchwork of peoples

There was a new common purpose across the region, but there were many differences, too. The Middle East and North Africa is a mosaic of different peoples, faiths, and cultures. The region is home to, among others, Arabs, **Berbers**, Jews, Turks, and Persians. Islam is the largest religion, but it is divided between the followers of the **Sunni** and **Shi'a** branches, and several groups that broke off those branches. The other faiths, including Christians, are also divided. The types of government targeted in the Arab Spring vary from traditional monarchies to dictatorships.

A young man holds a sign that says "People Demand a new Constitution" during anti-government protests in Tahrir Square, Cairo, Egypt.

What kind of future?

Some people wanted a more **secular** society, in which religious affairs were separated from the state. They wanted more social freedoms such as those in Western countries. Other people were more inspired by the Islamic faith in their search for a new social order. Women from all groups played a big part in the protests. Most people agreed that they wanted change and prosperity, but could they share a vision of the future?

A political earthquake

The ongoing political unrest put a great strain on long-standing tensions within many Middle Eastern countries. It also created conflict with, and between, the governments of the powerful countries that had influenced politics in the region for so long. How could they protect their own interests in the region? Should they get involved?

In 2010, Tunisian rapper El Général performed "Rais Lebled" ("To the President"), a song about the injustice in Tunisia. The song became the anthem of the Arab Spring.

> "Mr President, your people are dead.
> So many people are eating from the garbage.
> There, you see what is happening in the country!
> Miseries are everywhere and people haven't found anywhere to sleep.
> I speak here in the name of the people who were wronged..."

A translated version of "Rais Lebled" ("To the President"), the 2010 song by Tunisian rapper El Général. It was addressed to Tunisian President Ben Ali.

TUNISIA, 2010-2014

In December 2010 in Sidi Bouzid, a city in Tunisia, a man named Mohamed Bouazizi set himself on fire to protest Tunisian living and working conditions. A university graduate, Bouazizi was forced to make his living selling vegetables. He protested when officials confiscated his vegetable cart, and later died from his burns.

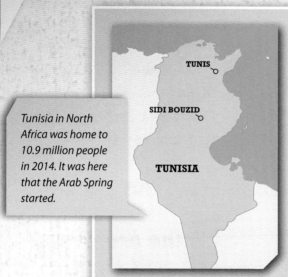

Tunisia in North Africa was home to 10.9 million people in 2014. It was here that the Arab Spring started.

NEWS FLASH

Name: Tunisian Republic
Capital: Tunis
Ethnic groups: Arabic, Berber, or Turkish descent 98%, also European and Jewish
Languages: Arabic, Shilha, and French
Religions: Islam 98%, Christianity, and Judaism
The back story:
• Ruled by France from 1881 to 1956
• President Habib Bourguiba ruled the country as a one-party state for 31 years.
• Zine el Abidine Ben Ali ruled from 1987 to 2011. He allowed other political parties, but made sure that only his party could win.

The first revolution

Bouazizi's single act triggered what became known as the Jasmine Revolution, or the Tunisian Revolution. This in turn sparked the Arab Spring. In a pattern that would repeat itself across the region in the coming months, protestors throughout Tunisia poured into streets to speak against rising prices, **corruption**, and **human rights** abuses. President Ben Ali had been in power for 23 years. Within a month of the protests, he was removed from office. Ben Ali fled to Saudi Arabia and the Tunisians rejoiced. However, the Tunisians continued to protest until all parts of the previous government had gone.

In Washington D.C., supporters of the Arab Spring protests held up a list of the leaders (described as "tyrants") they wanted to see removed from power, headed by Tunisia's Ben Ali.

A fresh start?

An election was held in October 2011. The outcome was a **coalition government** led by the **moderate Islamist** party Ennahda. Ennahda was soon criticized by the **secularists** for being too easy on the Salafists, who were Sunni Muslim followers who wanted to bring in the Islamic legal system known as **Shari'a** (see page 20). In turn, many Islamists criticized Ennahda for being too secular.

Amid growing tensions, the political parties agreed in 2014 that Mehdi Jomaa would act as prime minister, and the Ennahda party would step down. A new progressive **constitution** was introduced in 2014, and the first free and fair election happened in late 2014, with Beji Caid Essebsi assuming office in December.

A young woman proudly waves the Tunisian flag as she makes her way to a polling station during Tunisia's free elections.

> "The people think that the problems will simply disappear after a revolution. But they don't, they only change."
>
> Tunisian President Moncef Marzouki, interviewed by *Deutsche Welle*, March 2013

BEHIND THE PROTESTS

The Arab Spring protests began with peaceful demonstrations. Many became violent when government forces tried to crush the rallies and protestors resisted or tried to fight back. Some protests, such as in Syria, grew into wars that are ongoing. Others ended when government leaders stepped down, such as in Tunisia, or were forced from office, such as in Egypt.

DEBATE

Is violence needed to achieve change through political protest?

YES
Even non-violent demonstrations often end in violence. When protesting against a brutal, oppressive regime, violence is necessary to combat violence and make real change happen.

NO
Violence does not make a country a better place to live. It only causes more problems and hurts innocent people. Only the moral force of non-violence can bring fundamental and lasting peace.

Powerful forces

Why did the uprisings across the Middle East and North Africa become so explosive and volatile? For many years in the Middle East and North Africa, people who spoke against their governments or monarchies were silenced. For example, activists were viewed as troublemakers by their governments and were jailed, killed, or banned from their countries for decades. This kind of oppression, where people are not free to say what they believe, and live in constant fear of imprisonment or death if they do, means that many will risk their lives to press for freedom. Governments will also use violence to avoid losing power

Back to basics

When reporting on the Middle East and North Africa, television news channels often focus on religious divisions, violence, and the actions of political parties. When attempting to uncover the reasons for unrest, the media often ignores the most basic issues—that people want a living wage and security on the streets. In some countries, **radical Islamists** have won support by providing free food in struggling neighborhoods.

Democracy and Freedom

The Arab Spring uprisings were a push for greater freedoms, social justice, and democracy—a system in which governments are made up of fairly elected representatives of all citizens. In some countries, leaders have stepped down, but protestors' demands for democratic governments, voted in by the people, have not yet been met in many countries.

A homeless person begs on the street in Midoun, Djerba, Tunisia. High levels of poverty and homelessness increased the feelings of frustration leading up to the Arab Spring.

DICTATORSHIP AND DEMOCRACY

For many centuries, countries in southwest Asia and North Africa were under the rule of the Ottoman Turks, then European empires. Struggles for independence were often followed by governments that suppressed human and civil rights, or the rights of all citizens to political freedom and social equality.

A changing society

The restless mood of the Arab Spring reflected huge social changes. In countries such as Tunisia, young men and women had become more educated than their parents.

Many were well qualified but were frustrated because only a few jobs matched their skills. Repressive governance by old men was not for them. Even in the home, traditional, strict family structures were beginning to break down.

Having seized power in 1969, Muammar Gaddafi ruled Libya as a dictatorship until he was overthrown in 2011.

Demanding a voice

Young people saw themselves more as individuals, and wanted choices in the way they lived. They demanded a system in which leaders were held responsible and their rights were respected. Demonstrators chanted and carried signs demanding democratic elections and more say in how their countries were run. The protestors did not always share political beliefs, but they all wanted a better quality of life.

Followers of Islam, the largest religion in the region, were also engaged in debate. The majority of people wanted the government to be influenced by Islam in some way, but held different views on how the influence should take place.

Many views, one state?

One aim of democratic government is to reconcile multiple, or **pluralist**, views within society. Would the uprisings bring people together, or drive them apart?

> "In the past I only focused on personal dreams but now I'm focusing on a national dream that we all share."
>
> Egyptian student Ahmed Raafat Amin, *BBC News* website

WANTING DEMOCRACY

A 2012 Global Attitudes survey by Pew Research found that a high proportion of people in predominantly Islamic countries wanted democratic government.

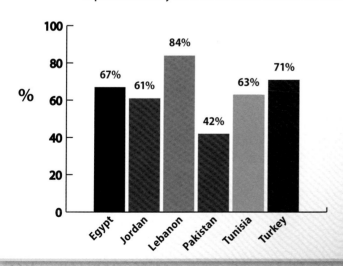

EGYPT, 2011-2016

Cairo, Egypt, is the biggest city in North Africa. It stands on the banks of the River Nile, a short distance from the ancient pyramids of Giza. At its center is Tahrir ("Liberation") Square, which became a global symbol of the Arab Spring.

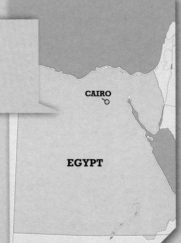

In 2014, there were approximately 86.9 million people living in Egypt.

CAIRO

EGYPT

NEWS FLASH

Name: Arab Republic of Egypt
Capital: Cairo
Ethnic groups: Egyptian 99.6%
Language: Arabic
Religions: Islam (90%), Coptic Christianity (9%), other Christianity (1%)
The back story:
• In 1952, Colonel Nasser led an overthrow of the Egyptian monarchy and seized power.
• Egypt was defeated in wars against Israel, but took control of the Suez Canal in 1956.
• President Anwar Sadat made peace with Israel in 1979, but was assassinated in 1981.

The rise of the people

In January 2011, about 50,000 protestors gathered in Tahrir Square, inspired by the news of the Jasmine Revolution in Tunisia. Within days, that number had grown to more than 300,000. Soon, protests spread to other cities. The public was excited by the possibility that change was at hand.

President Hosni Mubarak had held power for nearly 30 years. He had imprisoned people without trial, built secret detention centers, and failed to tackle corruption. He was now accused of allowing violent attacks to be made against the protestors. After just 18 days, Mubarak was forced to resign. He handed over power to the army, and was arrested.

Thousands of people packed into Tahrir Square, setting up makeshift camps, to protest against Mubarak's' regime.

"We are so furious. We must have change, better chances to work, to buy a flat, and have just the life's basics."

Protester in Tahrir Square, *BBC News*, 2011.

An experiment in democracy

In June 2012, the first truly democratic election in Egypt's history was narrowly won by Mohamed Morsi of the Freedom and Justice party, which was founded by the Islamist Muslim Brotherhood. Morsi was believed by many Western leaders to have moderate views, but he gave himself new powers and passed a new constitution that guaranteed some rights but favored Islamic fundamentalist beliefs. Protestors returned to Tahrir Square in a "Second Revolution."

The second downfall

The army was back in favor with the crowds. In June 2013, Morsi was forced from office and arrested. Some said the army was safeguarding the revolution. Others complained that this was a military **coup**. In March 2014, 529 supporters of the Muslim Brotherhood were sentenced to death. Abdel Fattah al-Sisi, the head of Egypt's armed forces and an instrumental member of the Morsi overthrow, was elected the new president in June 2014. Although unrest in Egypt has slowed, some groups say the human rights conditions have worsened under al-Sisi, with new protests and free speech being repressed.

Former President Hosni Mubarak was sentenced to life imprisonment, but this sentence was overturned. He was freed, but placed under house arrest.

IS DEMOCRACY ALWAYS GOOD?

Even though uprisings can create positive change in governments, democratic elections mean that usually, some groups of people are unhappy with the outcomes. The challenges faced by new democracies after the Arab Spring are not unique. Democracies have dealt with conflict, violence, and **civil wars** in many other regions.

People and power

Democracy has taken many different forms since it first developed in Greece about 2,500 years ago. It remains a far-from-perfect system. It may allow people to choose how they are governed, but it does not always ensure that the people's choice will be wise or moral. Even when a democracy has been in place for a long time, it may need to be rethought or reformed. This process can raise all sorts of **ethical** questions. Is democracy always good and dictatorship always wrong?

Can a dictator ever do good things for a country? Should political parties that reject the idea of equality for all be allowed to take part in a democratic election? For example, back in 1991, Algeria held its first democratic elections. When it became clear that an Islamist party would win, the army staged a coup to prevent the election from finishing. This resulted in 11 years of civil war. Is it ever okay to remove a democratic party from power by undemocratic means?

A Palestinian voting poll worker instructs a voter how to cast her ballot. Many Arab countries are now experiencing their first true democratic elections.

Even though his party was democratically elected, many people were unhappy with Mohamed Morsi's Muslim Brotherhood. After more protests, such as this one, the party was removed from power by the army.

"We don't want the Ikhwan [Muslim Brotherhood], and we don't want the old regime. We want a democratic state."

Egyptian novelist Alaa al-Aswany, The Guardian, 2013

DEBATE

Was Egypt's "Second Revolution" (see page 17) good for democracy?

(see page 17)

YES

President Mohamed Morsi had given himself too much power. His Islamist constitution took away rights. His overthrow led to a fair democratic election in 2014, in which Abdel Fattah al-Sisi was made president.

NO

The "revolution" was really a military takeover. The army should not arbitrarily oust a democratically-elected leader. In a democracy, people should use elections, rather than military force, to get rid of a party they do not like.

FAITH AND THE STATE

The first protestors of the Arab Spring were united in calling for economic and political change. However, events in Tunisia and Egypt opened up deep, political divides which led to unrest. Should the new states be based on religious or secular principles?

"I don't support the separation of religion and politics. If you apply Shari'a in the correct way, you gain prosperity and democracy..."

Egyptian Rasha Gamal, Aljazeera's news website, 2013

THE ISLAMIC CONTEXT

Some Muslims belong to strict sects, such as the Salafi movement, which reject the secular state. They call for full implementation of the Islamic moral and legal code known as Shari'a. While many aspects of Shari'a are compatible with a democratic state, others infringe on human rights (see pages 42–43) or advocate harsh forms of punishment such as lashing or stoning, which are unacceptable in a liberal democracy. Liberal democracy is a political ideology, or set of ideas, as well as a form of government. It operates under the belief that, among other things, every person should have the same political and social rights, and that governments should be freely elected.

Democratic Islam

Many different views and practices exist within Islam. Most followers of Islam regard the democratic process as legitimate, and they point out similarities with Islamic traditions, such as the key principle known as *Shura*, or consultation. Most Muslims follow their faith within diverse systems of government, and do not impose their religious beliefs.

Although the Islamists of the Arab Spring are often regarded with great suspicion by those who feel religion should be kept out of government, in the end both sides will have to compromise to find ways to live together.

Separating faith and state

Secularists are people who believe that the state, or government, should be kept separate from matters of personal faith. These people may or may not be religious themselves. Some of them see secularism itself as a good thing, while others see it more as a practical measure to avoid religious conflict within a nation.

Muslim women in Peshawar, a city in the north west of Pakistan, demonstrate their solidarity with the Muslim Brotherhood government in Egypt, carrying banners that proclaim their support.

LIBYA, 2011-2016

Muammar Gaddafi was the leader of Libya from 1969–2011, and many believed he was a dictator who ruled the country in fear. In February 2011, human rights campaigner Fathi Terbil was arrested, bringing protestors onto the streets of the large Libyan city of Benghazi. Although these events were common under Gaddafi's rule, this particular protest was part of the Arab Spring—and change was to come.

The population of the North African State of Libya was approximately 6.2 million people in 2014.

TRIPOLI
BENGHAZI
LIBYA

NEWS FLASH
Name: State of Libya
Capital: Tripoli
Ethnic groups: Libyan (Arab and Berber descent) 97%, others 3%
Languages Arabic, Berber languages, Italian, and English
Religions: Islam 97%, others 3%.
The back story:
• Independence from Italy granted in 1951.
• Muammar Gaddafi seized power in 1969.
• Gaddafi sponsored international terrorist attacks. The United States bombed Tripoli in 1986.
• After years of hostile relations and the killing of an ambassador, the U.S. now has a relationship with Libya.

Libya at war
The Libyan protests exploded into an uprising, which Gaddafi attacked with helicopters and guns. This sparked a civil war, which spread across Libya. In March 2011, the Security Council of the United Nations (UN) authorized a **no-fly zone** to protect the rebels from Gaddafi's air force.

French and British aircraft of the North Atlantic Treaty Organization (**NATO**) attacked Gaddafi's troops with missiles. Tripoli fell in August 2011, and the National Transitional Council (NTC) was recognized as Libya's new government. Gaddafi, in hiding, was killed by members of the NTC the following October.

The Libyan rebels consisted of civilians and army deserters who often had to use makeshift weapons and equipment in their battle against Gaddafi's Libyan army.

"They have no justification to put their hands on Libyan assets, other than as an act of theft and robbery..."

Muammar Gaddafi accuses the intervening NATO powers of seeking to profit from Libya's oil reserves, *Globe and Mail*, 2012

Ongoing conflict

The end of the 2011 civil war brought more violence and instability in Libya. Without an organized Libyan military to enforce change, **militias** with differing religious and political beliefs fought for control of the country. In September 2012, United States ambassador Chris Stevens and three other Americans were killed when an extremist Islamic militia attacked the American consulate building in Benghazi. Among disastrous human rights violations, the violence also crippled oil production, hurting Libya's economy. This violent climate led to a second civil war beginning in 2014, in which rival groups, including **ISIL**, are fighting to control the country. The war is ongoing, despite UN attempts to make peace.

A Libyan rebel shows the tunnel in the town of Sirte where Gaddafi was found and killed. Gaddafi ran into the tunnel to shelter from a NATO air strike.

RELIGIOUS OR SECULAR?

Should religion play a major role in government, or should the two be separated? This argument often has opposite extremes in opinion. In reality, the divisions between religion and state are often less clear-cut—neither complete integration, or mixing together, nor separation of religion and government exist.

The place of faith

The argument about secularism is often presented as a problem that happens mostly in the Middle East and North Africa, but it is common to many faiths and most parts of the world. In Europe and North America, there are many different constitutional arrangements and various, often changing, public attitudes toward religion. In the United States, for example, there are often disagreements between secularists and people who believe laws should follow Christian principles. Similarly, in the Middle East and North Africa, there are many secular and non-secular arrangements. For example, there is a huge difference between Saudi Arabia's strict enforcement of harsh

The laws in some countries do not allow Muslim women to choose whether to cover their faces. In liberal democracies, it is the choice that matters—whether women have the ability to freely choose what garments they wear and how they wish to follow their religious beliefs.

These unveiled Tunisian women hold up their ink-stained fingers, which show that they have voted in elections in October 2011. The country's government, as of 2016, is made up of cooperating secular and moderate Islamist parties.

religious law, and democratic Turkey where a moderate Islamist government works within a secular constitution.

Religious freedoms

The debate poses many questions. Should religious people respect the differing faiths—or lack of faith—of others? Should non-religious people always respect the rights of religious people? Should people be allowed to convert freely from one religion to another? Should religious laws made by a majority apply to members of a religious minority?

For some people, the answers to all these questions may have clear answers in holy scriptures. For others, it is a question of what they believe is just and right. In any democracy, the laws that define a state must enable conflicting views to coexist peacefully.

"Muslims, Christians, Jews— we are all Tunisians."

Translation of a secularist poster during Tunis protest in 2011

SAUDI ARABIA, 2011-2014

Saudi Arabia is the Arab heartland. Its land contains massive reserves of oil, making it an important economic region. Within the nation is the city of Mecca, the most holy city of Islam, which is visited each year by millions of people. Saudi Arabia is a very conservative and traditional country, following strict Islamic laws.

NEWS FLASH

Name: Kingdom of Saudi Arabia
Capital: Riyadh
Ethnic groups: Arabs 90%, Afro-Asian 10%
Languages: Arabic
Religions: Islam (Sunni 90%, Shi'a 10%)
The back story:
• Regions united to form the Kingdom of Saudi Arabia in 1932.
• Oil was discovered in 1938.
• In 2005, Abdullah bin Abdulaziz al-Saud became king. Saudi Arabia is an ally of the West, but there are concerns about Saudi terrorists.

The Kingdom of Saudi Arabia has an estimated population of more than 28.8 million people.

Challenging the system

When protests for human rights broke out in Saudi Arabia in 2011, they were met with arrests and shootings. The causes of the protests were many. Corruption was widespread. While the top families were incredibly wealthy, many ordinary people were poor, and unemployment was high. Political prisoners were locked away without trial. Women were denied equal rights with men. They could not vote, and were even forbidden to drive cars. Women began a Facebook campaign called Baladi, demanding the vote. In 2011, one woman

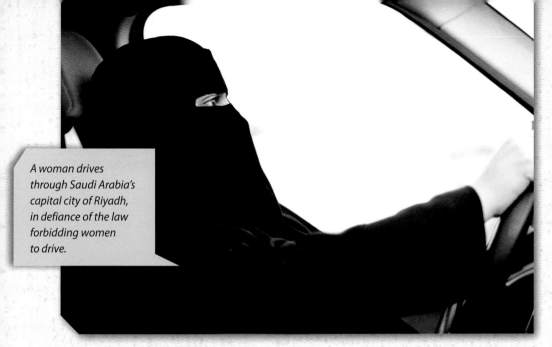

A woman drives through Saudi Arabia's capital city of Riyadh, in defiance of the law forbidding women to drive.

was sentenced to ten lashes, having been found guilty of driving a car. Fortunately, King Abdullah overturned the sentence.

Small steps to reform

King Abdullah maintained strict opposition to the Arab Spring protests, sending troops to Bahrain to help suppress the unrest there. However, he did give in to some of the demands at home. He increased the spending on welfare. He granted women the vote in city elections and in February 2013, 30 women were, for the first time, appointed to the Shura—the chief consultative council. Despite intimidation, arrest, and threats of harsh punishment, the brave protestors have not given up.

With the dramatic events unfolding in Syria and Egypt, it is easy to forget that the Arab Spring has set in motion many small but significant changes, although the conservative kingdom of Saudi Arabia is still considered to be far behind on their upholding of human rights.

King Abdullah, who allowed some important advancements in women's rights in the Kingdom of Saudi Arabia, died in 2015. His successor, King Salman, has upheld these decisions so far, but women still have a long way to go in achieving equal rights.

ELECTRONIC REVOLUTION

The events of the Arab Spring were extraordinary because once they started, the tide of change seemed to become unstoppable. Why was this revolution so widespread? One explanation is the prevalence of digital communication, with people spreading news by cell phone or over the Internet.

The rise of new technology

Media revolutions, such as printing technology or the rise of television, have gone hand-in-hand with political and social revolutions. These new electronic communications shaped the Arab Spring.

Radical networks

During the Arab Spring, change came quickest in countries with the highest use of digital media. Why was this? Texting, blogging, and social media sites can spread the word, helping to organize

THE E-SPRING

The first four months of 2011 saw the initial events of the Arab Spring. In that period:
• The region had 1.15 million people actively on Twitter, making 22,750,000 tweets. The most popular hashtags were "egypt" (1.4 million mentions), "jan25" (the day of the Egyptian revolution, with 1.2 million mentions), "libya"(990,000 mentions), "bahrain" (640,000 mentions) and "protest" (620,000 mentions).
• The number of Facebook users doubled (or more than doubled) in all Arab countries except Libya, when compared with the same period the year before.

demonstrations and making it possible to assemble protestors in a flash. Ordinary people, rather than journalists, can report and control the flow of news. This is sometimes considered more reliable than major news stations that can manipulate the information they present. Now, ordinary people can photograph or film events as they happen, and post them on sites such as YouTube.

Satellite vision

During the Arab Spring, video clips were then picked up by mainstream broadcasters. International broadcasters with strong regional connections, such as Aljazeera, which was founded in 1996, gave a voice to many activists. The Libyan rebels even set up their own Free Libya satellite station to counteract the state television channel.

Hosni Mubarak appeared on Arab news channel Aljazeera the day before he resigned. Rolling news coverage kept track of the fast-changing events as they happened across the Arab world.

"In the Arab world this winter, social media proved that it can facilitate rebellion and even topple regimes...Can social media help to build new governments?"

Don Tapscott, *The Huffington Post*, 2011

ACROSS BORDERS, 2011-2016

The Arab Spring had a big impact on many nations. Large protests and civil wars arose, and smaller protests were also held in countries such as Algeria and Sudan. The protests also had an influence on crises in other countries, such as Turkey, Lebanon, Iraq, Iran, Israel, and Palestine.

Name: Kingdom of Morocco
Languages: Arabic, Berber languages, and French
Religions: Islam 99%, Christian, and Jewish 1%

Name: Sultanate of Oman
Languages: Arabic, English, Baluchi, and Urdu
Religions: Ibadi Islam 75% and others (Sunni and Shi'a) 25%

Name: Republic of Yemen
Language: Arabic
Religions: Islam, small numbers of Christians, Jews, and Hindus

Name: Kingdom of Bahrain
Languages: Arabic, English, Farsi, Urdu
Religions: Islam (Sunni and Shi'a) 81%, Christian 9%, and others 10%

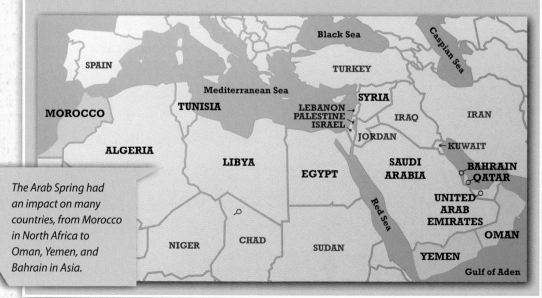

The Arab Spring had an impact on many countries, from Morocco in North Africa to Oman, Yemen, and Bahrain in Asia.

North Africa

Beginning on February 20, 2011, a group of mainly student protesters organized a series of demonstrations in Morocco. The group, known as the 20 February Movement, protested poverty, unemployment, **censorship**, and corruption in the country. The king, Mohammed VI, survived by avoiding confrontation. He drew up a new constitution, made political reforms, and held elections.

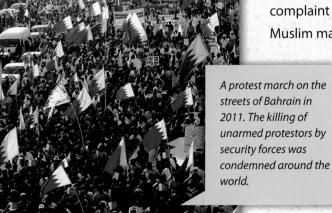

Protesters in Morocco were successful in bringing about change in their government's constitution and other political reforms.

In neighboring Algeria, early protests for better living conditions in the country were suppressed by the police, but began to simmer again in 2013. In 2016, the government announced its plan to complete the constitutional reforms proposed after the Arab Spring.

Around the Middle East

In 2011, crowds in Oman demanded freedom of speech, more job opportunities, better wages, and an end to corruption. They had some success: law-making powers were given to parliament, the minimum wage was raised, and a job-creation plan was promised.

In the same year, Yemen saw widespread city protests, but President Ali Abdullah Saleh repeatedly avoided stepping down. In June 2011, he was injured in an assassination attempt and was finally voted out in an election in February 2012.

In the small island state of Bahrain in the Persian Gulf, protests calling for human rights and freedoms began in 2011. Another complaint was the treatment of the Shi'a Muslim majority by the Sunni Muslim government. The police response was a brutal crackdown, with many protestors imprisoned and tortured. Protests still continue today.

A protest march on the streets of Bahrain in 2011. The killing of unarmed protestors by security forces was condemned around the world.

THE ROLE OF THE INTERNET

The forces driving the Arab Spring forward were social, economic, and political. The uprisings and protests were grassroots movements, meaning that they were driven by people who came together to demand political change. Social media, including Twitter and Facebook, was a major means of communicating the goals and actions of the protests.

"The Internet is becoming the town square for the global village of tomorrow."

Bill Gates, founder of Microsoft, 1999

Cyber rebels

The uprisings were made much more effective by the use of social media. People at protests could post images and videos of what was happening on the street and not worry about government sponsored media altering the message or hiding violence. This made them the reporters of their own news.

Some **authoritarian** countries, such as China, have tried to isolate their citizens from full access to the Internet by creating a national "firewall"—a computer system which controls the flow of information. However, the Internet is much harder to censor than printed media or television.

A demonstrator holds up a laptop showing images of celebrations in Cairo's Tahrir Square, after Egypt's president Hosni Mubarak resigned.

32

Power games

The Internet is useful as an engine of revolution and change. The Arab Spring is sometimes called the "Twitter Revolution" because people learned about the protests and the reasons behind them from Twitter posts made live by protestors. In Egypt, the government blocked Facebook and Twitter for a time and then blocked people's access to the Internet for five days. It believed shutting down access would stop the protests, but it didn't.

DEBATE
Should national agencies have the right to monitor private communications?

YES

*It allows authorities to prevent terrorism or other crimes by intercepting **perpetrators' plans**, therefore ensuring safety of citizens.*

NO

This is a privacy violation and, in the hands of a tyrant or dictator, could control the population—making future "Arab Springs" less likely.

Protestors in Istanbul in 2013 organized demonstrations quickly using the Internet and social media outlets such as Facebook and Twitter.

SYRIA, 2011–2016

After 15 students were imprisoned in Syria for writing anti-government statements on a wall in March 2011, major protests began in the ancient capital of Damascus, as well as in the cities of Aleppo and Daraa. Within days, hundreds of thousands of people were out on the streets. Violent civil war soon began.

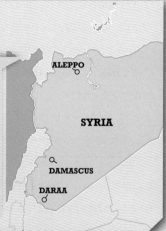

ALEPPO

SYRIA

DAMASCUS

DARAA

*Since the war began in 2011, an estimated 4.8 million registered Syrian refugees have been forced to flee their country. Another 6.5 million are **displaced** within Syria.*

NEWS FLASH

Name: Syrian Arab Republic
Capital: Damascus
Ethnic groups: Arabs 90%, Kurds, Armenians and others 10%
Languages: Arabic, Kurdish, Armenian, and Aramaic
Religions: Islam 90% and Christian 10%
The back story:
• The Syrian kingdom was occupied by France, which ruled until 1946.
• In 1970, Hafez al-Assad seized power.
• In 2000, his son Bashar al-Assad became president.

A long nightmare

To counter the protests, the government began a brutal crackdown. President Assad launched devastating attacks on his own cities with tanks and aircraft. Many soldiers left to join the uprising, forming the Free Syrian Army. Bids for peace brokered by the **Arab League** and the United Nations both failed. The rebels formed a Syrian National Council, but there were 13 larger and an estimated 1,200 smaller groups who had their own agenda. Both sides committed atrocities. Many foreign Islamist fighters came to join the rebels, who were armed by Qatar and Saudi Arabia. The Syrian government was supported by Iran and Russia. By 2014, Islamic State of Iraq and Levant (ISIL) had

SYRIAN REFUGEES

The UNHCR is also known as the UN Refugee Agency. It works alongside many other UN and independent agencies to care for those escaping from the civil war in Syria.

- Lebanon has 1,948,275 refugees
- Jordan has 589,000 refugees
- Turkey has 2,743,397 refugees

Other refugees are in Egypt, Iraq, North Africa, Europe, and North America.

Even though millions of Syrian people have already fled the country, millions more still carry out their lives amid the rubble.

claimed some of Syria's war-torn territory. The United States and other western countries intervened, supporting the rebels and taking action against ISIL.

The refugee crisis

By 2016, more than 11 million people had lost their homes and death toll estimates range from 250,000, to 470,000 people. The ongoing war means that the lives of Syrian people are at risk every day. An estimated 13.5 million Syrians needed humanitarian assistance because of the civil war. Many have made the difficult decision to flee their homes for safety outside of Syria. Refugee camps in nearby countries, such as Turkey and Lebanon, hold thousands of Syrian refugees. The living conditions in the camps are difficult. Some Syrian refugees have made dangerous journeys to Europe, where countries such as Germany have given them a safe home. Others are beginning to find safety in North America. However, the refugee crisis is still a major issue today. There are more refugees than some countries can—or are willing to—take in.

> "People burning in front of you. People dying. People running. But where will they run to? They're not safe anywhere. This is the fate of the Syrian people."
>
> Headmaster of a school hit by a bomb, Aleppo, *BBC News, 2013*

BEYOND THE REGION

The Middle East and North Africa have long been the focus of international rivalry. Powerful nations, such as the United States, Russia, China, France, and Britain, historically worked to gain control in the region's countries, often through force, threats, and violence.

The big players

The Middle East has always been a crossroads of trade in items the rest of the world desired, from spices in the Middle Ages to petroleum today. The region's rich oil resources attracted many European and western countries in the 1900s. Some colonized the area to control resources. Others formed alliances with elites within the region in order to ensure their oil supply needs were met. Some of these countries have also made millions selling **arms** to Arab countries.

War and terrorism left nations across the region devastated. Two troubled political arenas repeatedly threatened world peace: relations between Israel and the occupied Palestinian territories, in which conflict over borders has resulted in repeated wars and clashes. The tensions between Iran and the West, the wars in Iraq, and ongoing terrorist threats within some countries, have also made the region more volatile.

A Palestinian youth waves a flag while confronting Israeli soldiers in one of the occupied Palestinian territories.

ARMS FOR THE MIDDLE EAST AND NORTH AFRICA

Are international arms keeping the peace, or encouraging conflict? According to Amnesty International, in the five years before the Arab Spring broke out, 20 nations including Italy, France, Serbia, Switzerland, and the United States sold more than $2.4 billion worth of small arms, tear gas and armored vehicles to Bahrain, Egypt, Libya, Syria, and Yemen.

- 2010–2012: The United States gave $1.3 billion to Egypt each year to buy weapons from American companies.
- 2012: Russia announced that it would continue to sell arms to Syria, despite the civil war.
- 2013: A $6.8-billion American arms deal with Saudi Arabia was announced.
- 2013: A $4-billion American arms deal with United Arab Emirates was announced.
- 2013: The United States and United Kingdom resumed arms sales to Egypt as President Morsi was put on trial.

The popular challenge

The Arab Spring uprisings threatened to change the whole balance of power in the region. Egypt and Saudi Arabia had always been important allies of the United States. Syria was an ally of Russia and Iran. Would the whole system collapse? What would be the long-term effects of the uprisings? Who would benefit?

How to respond?

The response of Western governments and media was diverse. They applauded the Arab Spring, they criticized it, they supported some factions and not others, they called for democracy, and they expressed concern over the rise of a radical political Islam. Above all, they wondered if they should intervene to affect the outcome.

Russian president Vladimir Putin talks to Hosni Mubarak in April 2005. The world's major powers, including Russia and the United States, have gone to great lengths to develop relationships with various Arab nations.

SHOULD OTHER COUNTRIES ACT?

Western democracies say they want a stable Middle East. But do their calls for democracy in the Middle East and North Africa sound hollow, given their history of colonialism, imperialism, and military intervention in the region?

Hypocrisy—or the real world?

Over the years, the United States and its allies have supported dictators in many parts of the Middle East and North Africa. In 1953, Britain and the United States staged a coup in Iran to overthrow a democratically elected prime minister, Mohammad Mossadegh, because he had tried to take Iran's oil fields out of foreign ownership. This act had a lasting effect on Iranian politics and the relationship between Iran and the West.

The United States and Britain support democracy, but overthrew a democratic leader for their own benefit. Is this a double standard that undermines the case for democracy? Or is foreign intervention necessary to bring peace and stability to a region so that a healthy democracy can eventually flourish? Who benefits from foreign intervention? Are citizens of western democracies responsible for the actions of their governments—whom they democratically elected—in foreign lands?

DEBATE
Can democracy be imposed on another nation by force?

YES
Nations have a duty to ensure that other peoples can live free of tyranny. Human rights know no borders.

NO
By definition, democracy cannot be a system forced on others. It can succeed only if it comes from the people in the street.

Standing alone

A policy of not intervening in the affairs of other countries is called **isolationism**. In some situations a policy of isolationism may be reasonable, but in others less so. For example, the United States chose not to enter World War II until 1941, when it came under direct attack at Pearl Harbor. Some believe the conflict could have ended sooner if war was declared earlier.

Getting involved

In the 2000s, the United States and its allies intervened in Afghanistan and Iraq. They aimed to overthrow regimes that were abusing human rights. Critics were suspicious. They believed the intervention could have been motivated by a desire for power in the oil-rich region. In the end, both wars were seen by many as costly failures. This made some Western politicians reluctant to intervene in the civil wars during the Arab Spring. Does intervention make bad situations worse? Should **diplomacy** always come first?

> "...we have to stand with those who are working every day to strengthen democratic institutions, defend universal rights, and drive inclusive economic growth."
>
> Former US Secretary of State Hillary Clinton, 2011

Protestors outside the White House appeal for action against Syria after the use of chemical weapons against the Syrian people.

YELAN ROHAK YA HAFEZ
MULE

COPING WITH CRISIS

What can be done by the wider world to make dictators answer for their actions, to resolve conflicts such as civil war, to encourage diplomacy, or to promote human rights? A framework of international law controls the relations between countries.

International safeguards

Any international intervention in the affairs of a nation has to be agreed on by the United Nations (UN). Founded in 1945, today the UN has 193 full member countries, which together form a General Assembly. Key decisions are discussed by a Security Council, whose permanent members represent the world's most powerful countries. Each member has the right to veto, or reject, a proposal. This often results in stalemate and inaction.

Syrian refugees are shown here outside of their famil[y] tent in a Turkish refugee camp. Turkey has taken in the vast majority of peopl[e] (almost 3 million) fleeing the war in Syria that bega[n] with an Arab Spring prote[st]

Disagreement within the Security Council held up military intervention in Syria, to the anger and frustration of many. However, delay may also provide a check against overly quick action by member states. For example, humanitarian organizations such as the International Committee of the Red Cross believed that early proposals to intervene in Syria would have made a terrible situation even worse.

The big picture

UN agencies deal with a wide range of the concerns and issues raised by the Arab Spring, from economic development to human rights and the care of refugees.

Multinational and regional organizations, such as the Arab League or the African Union, may also take part in diplomacy or conflict resolution. The International Criminal Court (ICC), which is based in Netherlands, is independent of the UN and aims to bring to justice those accused of war crimes and other crimes against humanity.

Working internationally is extremely difficult and the options of all these organizations are limited and sometimes ineffective. However, without them, there would be little hope for those rising up against injustice.

> **"About 40 percent of the population [in Syria]—now needs outside assistance."**
>
> Valerie Amos, UN humanitarian chief, *BBC News*

THINKING ABOUT HUMAN RIGHTS

The issue of human rights is common throughout all of the uprisings in the Middle East and North Africa. Human rights refer to the basic requirements that everyone on the planet needs to lead a happy and healthy life. However, not all people may agree on the basic requirements that are needed.

DEBATE — Should all human beings have the same human rights?

YES

Human rights are universal ideas. They apply to all people in the world equally, regardless of their cultural or religious background.

NO

Human rights have different meanings depending on their context. Their definition may differ according to the religious and cultural traditions of one's society.

Declaring your rights

Many nations have their own bill or charter of constitutional rights. In 1948, the UN adopted a Universal Declaration of Human Rights (UDHR). In its present form, this declaration addresses many of the concerns of the Arab Spring, such as equality, liberty, security, wrongful arrest and detention, a fair legal process, freedom of thought and expression, religious freedom, the right to work for a fair wage, and the right to receive education.

Some people criticize the UDHR, saying that it is based too heavily on Western tradition and does not allow for cultural or religious difference. In 1990, the 57 member states of the Organization of

The UN has offices around the world, such as this one in Geneva, Switzerland.

42

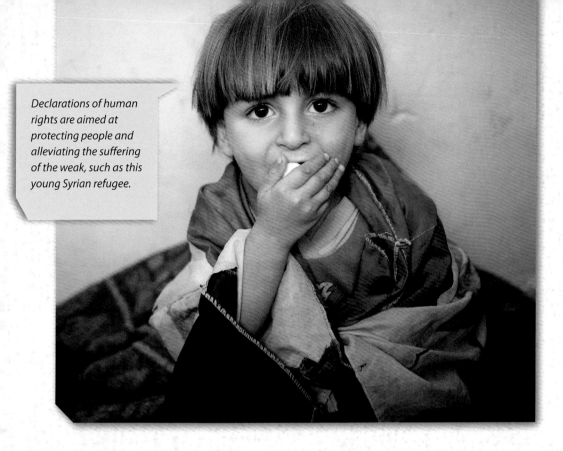

Declarations of human rights are aimed at protecting people and alleviating the suffering of the weak, such as this young Syrian refugee.

Islamic Cooperation (OIC) drew up an alternative document, the Cairo Declaration of Human Rights in Islam (CDHRI). Based on Shari'a, it shares some common ground with the UDHR and also supports many of the aims and claims of the Arab Spring. However, it is based on a single religion and it differs from the UDHR on some of the basic issues, such as religious freedom and equality, freedom of expression, the rights of women, and the nature of punishment. These are the same issues that have often caused division between secularists and Islamists. The Cairo Declaration has been strongly criticized by the International Commission of Jurists, an international group of experts who advise on human rights, who feel that the CDHRI's focus on religion can be harmful to human rights.

"All human beings are born free and equal in dignity and rights. They are endowed with reason and conscience and should act towards one another in a spirit of brotherhood."

Article I, Universal Declaration of Human Rights (UDHR)

ON TO THE FUTURE

In 2011, young protestors across the Middle East and North Africa felt hopeful. They were changing the world. Today, the strife in Libya and other countries has made many people question the Arab Spring. The conditions in Syria are also shocking the world. Was it all in vain?

Shifting sands

The Arab Spring did upset the big power alliances across the region, and the Middle East and North Africa are undergoing a period of change. However, political change is rarely delivered quickly and neatly, especially if those in revolt have different, often conflicting, interests. As many countries have seen, unseating an oppressive ruler does not always result in a healthy democracy. Disappointments and setbacks are inevitable and violence is all too likely.

Lessons to be learned

The failures of the Arab Spring have become all too obvious since 2013. However, the protests' successes are also important. Ordinary people have proven that their voices matter, and that their human rights are important—even if it means overthrowing a ruler or engaging in violence. The foundations of the Middle East and North Africa have been shaken by a tremor. Many more may follow.

Many people are still living in countries torn apart by conflict or are having to cope with years of violent strife.

After the initial wave of euphoria following the Arab Spring, many countries are now facing up to the hard work necessary to bring about change.

"It is the first time we have been so united since the revolution. It is like another revolution."

Asma Habaib, a bank worker in central Tunis, celebrates the new democratic Tunisian constitution of 2014

GLOSSARY

Arab League
An organization of 22 Arab countries in North Africa and the Middle East

Arab Spring
A term describing the series of protests and uprisings across North Africa and the Middle East that began in Tunisia in 2010

arms
Weapons and ammunition

authoritarian
Describing a system in which individuals are expected to obey authority over their will

Berber
A group of people native to North Africa

censorship
Blocking or altering forms of communication or media on the grounds of politics, morality, religious teaching, or other concerns, such as national security

civil war
A war fought between various groups within the same country

coalition government
A government created in the absence of a majority, in which multiple political parties cooperate with each other

Cold War
From 1945 to 1989, the state of nonviolent hostility between the United States and the former U.S.S.R., now Russia

colonialism
when one country or empire takes control of a territory and its resources and often, settles its people on the land

constitution
The principles and legal framework on which a state or an entire nation is established and governed

corruption
Dishonest or illegal actions by those in power

coup
Short for *coup d'état*, it is any sudden and decisive political action, especially the seizure of governing power by non-democratic means

demilitarize
To remove military forces from an area

dictatorship
Oppressive, undemocratic rule by a single person, military leader, or party

diplomacy
The practice, profession, or skill of maintaining good international relationships

displaced
The act of being forced from one's home

ethical
Something that is based upon moral principles

human rights
Provisions or principles which aim to ensure that all humans have equal access to justice, freedom, and other essentials

imperialism
Where one country extends its power over others through government dealings or military force

intercept
To break into communications to read or listen to the message

ISIL
Short for Islamic State of Iraq and the Levant and also known as ISIS; a militant group that follows an extreme, fundamental branch of Islam and is known for its terrorist acts

Islamist
A term, which is rejected by some Muslims, that describes the belief that countries should be run by the principles of Islam

isolationism
A national policy of not being drawn into any international involvement or intervention in a situation

militia
A fighting force that is made up of a collection of citizen volunteers or non-professional soldiers

moderate
Describing "middle ground" views that do not lean to one extreme or the other

NATO
Short for North Atlantic Treaty Organization; a military alliance which has 28 member states across North America and Europe

no-fly zone
An area where a nation or a group of nations is prevented from deploying aircraft during a war or military stand-off

oppressive
Describing a person, society, or government that inflicts unjust hardship, cruel treatment, or control on other people or groups of people

pluralist
Made up of several political parties or faiths

radical Islamists
Also known as Islamic fundamentalists, a movement of Muslims who want a return to the fundamentals of the religion

refugee
A person who flees to a foreign country because they have a legitimate reason to fear their safety in their home country

resistance
actions that bring pressure on a government to force it to change

revolution
A change in constitution, politics, or governments, sometimes involving an overthrow of one system to be replaced by another

secular
Referring to non-religious matters

secularist
Someone who wishes to keep matters of state or education free from religious influence

Shari'a
The framework of principles and laws within Islam; it is interpreted in many different ways, and some aspects may conflict with secular legal systems

Shi'a
One of the main religious groupings within Islam, in which religious leaders called imams interpret the teachings of the prophet Muhammad

Sunni
The largest grouping within the Islamic world, in which the Ummah or wider Islamic community plays an important part

INDEX